COME, LORD JESUS

Dr James Tolhurst is the Series Editor of the Newman Millennium Edition. His many books, also published by Gracewing, include studies on John Henry Newman and selections from Newman's writings, as well as *A Concise Catechism for Catholics*.

COME, LORD JESUS

Reflections on the Advent
and Christmas Seasons

James Tolhurst

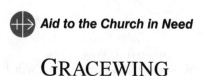

Aid to the Church in Need

GRACEWING

First published in 2006

Gracewing
2 Southern Avenue
Leominster
Herefordshire HR6 0QF

The right of James Tolhurst to be identified as the author of this
work has been asserted in accordance with the Copyright,
Designs and Patents Act 1988.

ISBN 0 85244 020 0
978 0 85244 020 9

Special edition printed by arrangement with
Gracewing Publishing for:
⊕Aid to the Church in Need
12–14 Benhill Avenue, Sutton, Surrey, SM1 4DA
Registered with the Charity Commission No. 1097984

Typeset by Action Publishing Technology Ltd,
Gloucester GL1 5SR

Printed in England by
Antony Rowe Ltd, Chippenham, Wiltshire

Contents

Introduction

When he writes about Advent, Pope Benedict XVI says that there are two main figures which dominate this liturgical time: John the Baptist and Mary.

John sees the coming of the Messiah coinciding with the Day of the Lord (cf. Isaiah 13:6). This 'Day' which we see as the Second Coming of Christ is the underlying theme of the thirty-second to the thirty-fourth weeks of the Church's liturgical year, leading into Advent. Originally *Advent* was the term used for the *Arrival* of the emperor in the province or of the deity on his festival. For Christianity, it signals God's presence in the world that will last until Christ comes again. These two themes have been combined in our liturgy: 'When the Church celebrates the liturgy of Advent each year, she makes present the ancient expectancy of the Messiah, for, by sharing in the long preparation for the Saviour's first coming, the faithful renew their ardent desire for his second coming.'[1] So, Wednesday the first week begins with the words: 'The Lord is coming and will not delay ...' The first Sunday of Advent (C) presents us with the doomsday scenario, of the End Times beginning: 'There will be signs in the sun, the moon and the stars, and on earth nations will be in dismay, perplexed by the roaring of the sea and the waves' (Luke 21:25).

But this is overlaid with the picture of the Messiah portrayed by the prophets, longed for by Israel. All the first scripture readings of the first ten days of Advent are from

---

[1] *Catechism of the Catholic Church* n. 524.

Isaiah, giving us the familiar descriptions of the expected Messiah. He will wield authority over the nations, hammering their swords into ploughshares. Many will come from East and West to the mountain of the Lord to take their place at the messianic banquet. Jesus is seen in the Gospel sequences as fulfilling the prophecies. He will feed the four thousand on the mountain. The eyes of the blind will see and Israel will feel the compassion of the Good Shepherd whose yoke is easy and whose burden is light. The message is brought to a conclusion on Tuesday of the second week with Isaiah's words: 'A voice cries, "Prepare in the wilderness a way for the Lord. Make a straight highway for our God across the desert."'

The voice will be that of John the Baptist who makes his appearance on Thursday of the second week. Jesus tells the crowd: 'of all the children born of women, a greater than John the Baptist has never been seen ... because it was towards John that all the prophecies of the prophets and of the Law were leading.' He will go on to explain that the prophecy on the return of Elijah to announce the coming of the Messiah is precisely fulfilled in John. Jesus would go on to compare himself with his cousin, saying that both would be rejected by a fickle crowd who wanted its prophets to conform to their criteria.

We are reminded that at the very end of his ministry, Jesus turned the argument of the chief priests about his own authority back on them by asking where John the Baptist's authority came from, heaven or man? He will finally tell John's disciples that he is the Messiah that they were expecting 'and happy is the man who does not lose faith in me'. He is no reed which bends before the wind – the conflict with Herod is just round the corner. He is the voice and the shining light which is praised by the Word and the Light of the World.

From 17 December, John the Baptist fades from the picture and Mary takes centre stage. We have the three annunciations by an angel: to Joseph that the Virgin will conceive and give birth to a son; to Zechariah and Elizabeth; and to Mary, that she is to be the Mother of God. The

2

first readings offer a type of commentary on the Gospels, as we have the narrative of the angel appearing to Manoah with the angel appearing to Zechariah; and the prophecy of the Lord speaking to Ahaz (that the maiden is with child and will soon give birth to Immanuel) with Gabriel's words to Mary. The *Magnificat* in which Mary manifests her humility is echoed by the prayer of Hannah, the mother of Samuel and the birth of John is introduced by the prophecy of Malachi in which Elijah is promised 'before my day comes'. Zechariah finally reminds us that God has indeed visited his people. So we are ready for the final scene of this liturgical drama when the decree goes out from Augustus to this forgotten corner of his empire, not knowing that he will be fulfilling the prophecy that the King of Kings will be born in David's royal city; and that, in the fullness of time a pope will live where he once ruled.

The Gospel is given for each day, with a short commentary. (In the case of Sundays, a choice has been made from the A, B and C cycles.) There is also a reading taken usually from the early writings of the Christian Church, and biographical details of the authors quoted, together with a concluding reflection.

May these reflections help you to prepare in mind and heart. We need this special time to pause in our hectic rush and realize that we are waiting for him who is the First and the Last, our Beginning and our End. May we echo the words of the Third Eucharistic Prayer and be 'ready to meet him when he comes again [offering] in thanksgiving this holy and living sacrifice'. We need also to hear the words of Jesus, 'happy is the one who does not lose faith in me'.

James Tolhurst 2006

First Sunday of Advent

Gospel: Matthew 24:37–44 (A)

Jesus said to his disciples: 'As it was in the days of Noah, so it will be at the coming of the Son of Man. In those days before the flood, they were eating and drinking, marrying and giving in marriage, up to the day that Noah entered the ark. They did not know until the flood came and carried them all away. So will it be also at the coming of the Son of Man. Two men will be out in the field; one will be taken, and one will be left. Two women will be grinding at the mill; one will be taken and one will be left. Therefore, stay awake! For you do not know on which day your Lord will come. Be sure of this: if the master of the house had known the hour of night when the thief was coming, he would have stayed awake and not let his house be broken into. So too, you also must be prepared, for at an hour you do not expect, the Son of Man will come.'

| ♦ |

In the second reading for this Sunday St Paul reminds the Christians of Rome that the Day of the Lord is near: 'It is the hour now for you to awake from sleep. For our salvation is nearer now than when we first believed' (Romans 13:11).

There is some discussion as to how widespread was the belief that the end times were just around the corner. St Paul would tell the Thessalonians that they shouldn't get disturbed by rumours that the time was at hand (2 Thessalonians 2:2). But since people were thinking on these lines, Paul would remind them that there was no excuse to grow lax. If that Day was coming, they should not behave like 'night people': 'let us conduct ourselves properly as in the day.'

Jesus, who has entered Jerusalem on a donkey and proph-esied that the Temple would be destroyed, provides a series of pictures/parables reminding people of the suddenness of that Day, 'so you too, you also must be prepared'. Are we ready to meet the Lord each time we receive the Eucharist; for 'in these *last days* [God] spoke to us through a son, whom he made heir of all things and through whom he created the universe' (Hebrews 1:2).

———————— ♦ ————————

How blessed, how fortunate, are those servants whom the Lord will find watchful when he comes. Blessed is the time of waiting when we stay awake for the Lord, the Creator of the universe, who fills all things and transcends all things.

How I wish he would awaken me, his humble servant, from the sleep of slothfulness, even though I am of little worth. How I wish he would enkindle me with that fire of divine love. The flames of his love burn beyond the stars; the longing for his overwhelming delights and the divine fire ever burn within me!

St Columbanus, *An Instruction on Compunction* # 12

Saint Columbanus, Abbot (c.540–615)
He was born in Leinster, Ireland and became a monk and disciple of Congall of Bangor. He left with twelve companions for Gaul in 590 and founded a monastery at Annegray in Austrasia and later at Luxeuil in the Vosges. He eventually established the famous monastery at Bobbio and died there on 23 November.

| ♦ |

Bestow upon me, O Gracious, O Holy Father:
A heart to meditate upon you,
Eyes to hear you,
A tongue to proclaim you,
A conversation pleasing to you,
Patience to wait for you,
And perseverance to look for you.
Grant me a perfect end – your holy Presence.
St Benedict (c.480–547)

5

Monday First Week of Advent

Gospel: Matthew 8:5–11

When Jesus went into Capernaum a centurion came up and pleaded with him. 'Sir,' he said, 'my servant is lying at home paralysed, and in great pain.' 'I will come myself and cure him,' said Jesus. The centurion replied: 'Sir, I am not worthy to have you under my roof; just give the word and my servant will be cured. For I am under authority myself, and have soldiers under me; and I say to one man: Go, and he goes; to another: Come here, and he comes; to my servant: Do this, and he does it.' When Jesus heard this he was astonished and said to those following him, 'I tell you solemnly, nowhere in Israel have I found faith like this. And I tell you that many will come from east and west to take their places with Abraham and Isaac and Jacob at the feast in the kingdom of heaven.'

| ♦ |

Matthew places the healing of the centurion's servant after the sermon of the mount, when Jesus returns to Capernaum.

It is one of the great miracles which we remember every time we celebrate the Eucharist, for we repeat the words of the centurion moments before Communion. The choice of Isaiah's particular prophecy owes much to Jesus' final phrase that many will come from all corners of the globe to take their place with the patriarchs at the feast in the kingdom. In his prophecy, the nations will stream to Jerusalem and the Lord will console his people. Jesus will extend the prophecy to include those who are not formally members of the Chosen People – the centurion is one 'who loved our nation and built the synagogue' (Luke 7:5).

Listen to the words of St Paul: 'Let a man examine himself, and so eat the bread and drink of the cup. For anyone who eats and drinks without discerning the body, eats and drinks judgement upon himself. That is why many of you are weak and ill, and some have died' (1 Corinthians 11:28–31). Do you now understand how illness and death often come about, on approaching the divine mysteries unworthily.

You may be inclined to say, 'But who is worthy?' I too am aware of this difficulty. And, nevertheless, you need to desire such worthiness. Recognize yourself to be a sinner, distance yourself from sin, flee from evil and anger. Practise works of penance. Review your attitude towards self-discipline, humility and patience. Compassion and heartfelt mercy for the needy are the fruits of justice. Practise these and you will have made yourself worthy.

St Anastasius Sinaita (d. *c.*700), *Sermon on the Holy Synaxis*

St Anastasius Sinaita (d. c.700)
Abbot of the monastery of St Catherine on Mt Sinai. He was a theologian and writer on the person and work of Christ. His principal work was *Hodegos* (Guide), a defence of the faith directed at those who held heterodox opinions about the Incarnation. He was known as the 'the new Moses'.

| ♦ |

O Lord, I am not worthy that should should'st come to me;
But speak the word of comfort, my spirit healed shall be.
And humbly I'll receive the bridegroom of my soul,
No more by sin to grieve thee or fly thy sweet control.

O Herr, ich bin nicht würdig (1777)

Tuesday First Week of Advent

Gospel: Luke 10:21–24

Filled with joy by the Holy Spirit, Jesus said: 'I bless you Father, Lord of heaven and earth, for hiding these things from the learned and the clever and revealing them to mere children. Yes, Father, for that is what it pleased you to do. Everything has been entrusted to me by my Father; and no one knows who the Son is except the Father, and who the Father is except the Son and those to whom the Son chooses to reveal him.

Then turning to his disciples he spoke to them in private, 'Happy the eyes that see what you see, for I tell you that many prophets and kings wanted to see what you see, and never saw it, to hear what you hear, and never heard it.'

| ♦ |

Jesus had just welcomed back the seventy-two disciples from their mission. They return, buoyed up with the success of their preaching and their healing to be told that they should rather rejoice that their names are written in heaven.

Matthew then inserts Jesus' reflections on the qualities required to inherit that kingdom, which are possessed by the childlike. Isaiah in his prophecy has a little child leading a calf and lion cub and putting his hand in the viper's lair: such is the time of innocence. Jesus will comment that intellect will not guarantee that we enter into the kingdom prepared for us, unless we have that faith which is willing to entrust itself totally to God.

Christ loves childhood. He himself has lived through it in body and soul. Christ loves childhood, mistress of humility, norm of innocence, model of sweetness ... He directs the behaviour of adults towards it ... He attracts by his example those whom he raises to the eternal kingdom.

But if we want to be able to understand perfectly how it is possible to come to such an admirable conversion, and what kind of transformation we have to undergo to reach the age of childhood, let us allow St Paul to instruct us. He says: 'Do not be children in your thinking; be babes in evil, but in thinking be mature' (1 Corinthians 14:20).

St Leo, *Sermon 7 on the Epiphany*

St Leo the Great (d. 461)
He became Pope in 440. He stated the doctrine of the Incarnation at the Council of Chalcedon in 451, when the delegates claimed 'Peter has spoken by the voice of Leo'. He mediated with the Vandals and the Huns in order to save the city of Rome and was declared a Doctor of the Church in 1754.

| ♦ |

Spiritual childhood is not spiritual foolishness or flabbiness; it is a sane and forceful way which, due to its difficult easiness, the soul must begin and continue, led by the hand of God.

St Josemaría Escrivá (1902–1975)

Wednesday First Week of Advent

Gospel: Matthew 15:29–37

Jesus reached the shores of the Sea of Galilee, and he went up into the hills. He sat there, and large crowds came to him bringing the lame, the crippled, the blind, the dumb and many others; these they put down at his feet, and he cured them. The crowds were astonished to see the dumb speaking, the cripples whole again, the lame walking and the blind with their sight, and they praised the God of Israel.

But Jesus called his disciples to him and said, 'I feel sorry for all these people; they have been with me for three days now and have nothing to eat. I do not want to send them off hungry, they might collapse on the way.' The disciples said to him, 'Where could we get enough bread in this deserted place to feed such a crowd?' Jesus said to them, 'How many loaves have you?' 'Seven,' they said 'and a few small fish.' Then he instructed the crowd to sit down on the ground, and he took the seven loaves and the fish, and he gave thanks and broke them and handed them to the disciples who gave them to the crowds. They all ate as much as they wanted, and they collected what was left of the scraps, seven baskets full.

| ♦ |

Isaiah talks of the banquet of rich food which the Messiah will prepare, 'for the hand of the Lord rests on this mountain.' It is the theme which Jesus takes up in his parable of the great feast (Luke 14:15–24).

In Matthew's Gospel, the 'banquet' is in the form of the feeding of the four thousand, when, as it says 'he went up into the hills ...' The context of such a banquet (as well as the feeding of the five thousand) is clearly, according to St John, the feeding *by God*, of the children of Israel with the manna, during their time in the wilderness. At the same time, John calls attention to the fact that the crowd drew the conclusion and wanted to acclaim Jesus as King (John 6:15).

All that is said and done on Corpus Christi is actually just a variation of what love is and what it does. In one of his hymns for the feast, Thomas Aquinas has found the following beautiful formula for this theme: *nec sumptus consumitur*: love does not consume, it gives; and in giving, it receives. In giving it is not emptied, but renews itself. Corpus Christi is a profession of love ...

Pope Benedict XVI, from *The Feast of Faith*

Great and indeed venerable is the fact that manna rained upon the Jews from heaven. But understand! What is greater, manna from heaven or the body of Christ? Surely the body of Christ, who is the Author of heaven. Further, he who ate the manna died; he who has eaten this body will gain remission of sins and shall not die forever.

St Ambrose (339–397)

Thursday First Week of Advent

Gospel: Matthew 7:21.24–27

Jesus said to his disciples: 'It is not those who say to me: "Lord, Lord", who will enter the kingdom of heaven, but the person who does the will of my Father in heaven.

'Therefore, everyone who listens to these words of mine and acts on them will be like a sensible man who built his house on rock. Rain came down, floods rose, gales blew and hurled themselves against that house, and it did not fall: it was founded on rock. But everyone who listens to these words of mine and does not act on them will be like a stupid man who built his house on sand. Rain came down, floods rose, gales blew and struck that house, and it collapsed and was completely ruined.'

| ♦ |

Isaiah proclaims that the Lord 'is the everlasting Rock' who will humble the mighty even to the dust.

Jesus has proclaimed the Beatitudes, and in St Matthew we are given a series of proverbial observations: 'No one can serve two masters, the lamp of the body is the eye, enter through the narrow gate ...' He concludes with this parable about the true and lasting foundation for those who would enter the kingdom. Just as he would name Simon, the Rock, so he would urge people to put a sure base for their life 'for he taught them as one having authority, and not as their scribes' (Matthew 7:29).

If we construct a temple by our own efforts it would not last; it is not held together by the teachings of this world or by our own feeble efforts or anxieties. We must build and preserve it by other methods. It must not have its foundations on earth or on sand which turn out to be unstable and treacherous. It must be built up from living stones, pinned together by the corner-stone and so it will grow into that perfect stature to the scale of Christ's body ... Such a house so built by God, will not collapse.

St Hilary, *Treatise on Psalm 126*

St Hilary (315–368)
His pagan parents were wealthy. He became an orator, married and had a daughter, Afra. After much study he was baptized, championed the cause of orthodoxy, and eventually became Bishop of Poitiers in 353. He was described as 'the Athanasius of the West', but was exiled by the Emperor for several years, to Asia Minor.

| ♦ |

Lord, grant that I may always allow myself to be guided by you, always follow your plans and perfectly accomplish your holy will. Grant that in all things, great and small, today and all the days of my life, I may do whatever you require of me. Help me respond to the slightest prompting of your grace so that I may be your trustworthy instrument for your honour. May your will be done in time and in eternity – by me, in me and through me.

St Teresa of Avila (1515–1582)

Friday First Week of Advent

Gospel: Matthew 9:27–31

As Jesus went on his way two blind men followed him shouting, 'Take pity on us, Son of David.' And when Jesus reached the house the blind men came up with him and he said to them: 'Do you believe that I can do this ?' They said: 'Sir, we do.' Then he touched their eyes saying: 'Your faith deserves it, so let this be done for you.' And their sight returned. Then Jesus sternly warned them, 'Take care that no one learns about this.' But when they had gone, they talked about him all over the countryside.

| ♦ |

When the Messiah comes the deaf will hear and the eyes of the blind will see. This literally comes true when Zechariah recovers his voice at his son's birth (Luke 1:64).

Matthew has Jesus 'passing on' from Capernaum, after healing the paralytic and raising the official's daughter to life. Two blind men follow him on the road. Some believe that this incident which is repeated in chapters 20:29–34 is placed here to anticipate the answer that Jesus would give to John the Baptist's disciples in chapter 11. Telling people not to talk about their miraculous cure belongs to Jesus' wish not to be recognized as the Messiah, until the climatic moment before the High Priest (Matthew 26:57).

When speaking about praying, it is very useful to keep oneself in the presence of God and to speak with him as one converses with a friend who is physically present. Just as images which are stored in the memory give rise to thoughts when those figures are thought about in the mind, so too we believe that it is useful to recall God present in the soul. He controls all our movements, even the slightest ones, when we are willing to show gratitude to the one we know to be present within us, to this God who examines the heart and scrutinizes the thoughts.

Origen, *Treatise on Prayer*

Origen (185–253)
He was probably born in Alexandria. He replaced Clement as Director of the Catechetical School. In 231 he founded a school of theology at Caesarea at the request of the bishop. He brought Bishop Beryllus of Bostia back to the faith and was imprisoned under the persecution of the Emperor Decius and probably died under torture. He has not however been canonized.

| ♦ |

To pray generously is not enough; we must pray devoutly, with fervour and piety. We must pray perseveringly and with great love.

Blessed Teresa of Calcutta (1910–1997)

Saturday First Week of Advent

Gospel: Matthew 9:35–37; 10:1, 5–8

Jesus made a tour through all the towns and villages, teaching in their synagogues, proclaiming the Good News of the kingdom and curing all kinds of diseases and sickness.

And when he saw the crowds he felt sorry for them because they were harassed and dejected, like sheep without a shepherd. Then he said to his disciples, 'The harvest is rich but the labourers are few, so ask the Lord of the harvest to send labourers to his harvest.'

He summoned his twelve disciples, and gave them authority over unclean spirits with power to cast them out and to cure all kinds of diseases and sickness. These twelve Jesus sent out, instructing them as follows: 'Go rather to the lost sheep of the House of Israel. And as you go, proclaim that the kingdom of heaven is close at hand. Cure the sick, raised the dead, cleanse the lepers, cast our devils. You received without charge, give without charge.'

| ♦ |

The theme of the Gospel is summed up by Isaiah: 'You will live in Jerusalem and weep no more.' God will have mercy on his people and dress their wounds.

Jesus looks out on the crowds with great compassion, not simply because most are poor and hungry but because they were 'harassed and dejected, like sheep without a shepherd'. He saw their hunger for the word of God and the need for labourers to go and give them that word. They did not need all the legalisms of the scribes, or the righteousness of the Pharisees or the timeserving of the Sadducees but the true and uplifting message which gives life and hope.

Let us listen to what the Lord says as he sends the preachers forth: 'The harvest is great but the labourers are few. Pray therefore the Lord of the harvest to send labourers into his harvest.' We can speak only with a heavy heart of so few labourers for such a great harvest for although there are many to hear the Good News there are only a few to preach it. Look about you and see how full the world is of priests, yet in God's harvest a labourer is rarely to be found; for although we have accepted the priestly office, we do not fulfil its demands ... I speak of our absorption in external affairs; we accept the duties of office, but by our actions we show that we are attentive to other things. We abandon the ministry of preaching and, in my opinion, are called bishops to our detriment, for we retain the honourable office but fail to practise the virtues proper to it.

St Gregory I, *Homily 17,3 The Performance of our Ministry*

St Gregory the Great (c.540–604)
He was the son of a Roman senator and followed his father into the civil administration. In 573 he sold his properties in order to endow six monasteries in Sicily and one in Rome on the Caelian Hill. He was made one of the seven deacons of Rome by Benedict I and later abbot of his monastery. As Pope he sent Augustine to England in 597. He concluded a peace with the Lombards and played an influential part in the development of the Roman liturgy. He was the first to use the title 'Servant of the servants of God'.

| ♦ |

Lord, fill with the gift of the Holy Spirit those whom you have called to the priesthood. Make them worthy to stand without blame at your altar, to proclaim your Gospel and to carry out your saving ministry by offering your sacrifice and sacraments to the holy people they are called to serve.

from the Byzantine Liturgy (adapted)

Second Sunday of Advent

Gospel: Matthew 3:1–12 (B)

The beginning of the Gospel of Jesus Christ the Son of God. As it is written in Isaiah the prophet: 'Behold, I am sending my messenger ahead of you; he will prepare your way. A voice of one crying out in the desert: 'Prepare the way of the Lord, make straight his paths.'

John the Baptist appeared in the desert proclaiming a baptism of repentance for the forgiveness of sins. People of the whole Judaean countryside and all the inhabitants of Jerusalem were going out to him and were being baptized by him in the Jordan river as they acknowledged their sins. John was clothed in camel's hair, with a leather belt around his waist. He fed on locusts and wild honey. And this is what he proclaimed: 'One mightier than I is coming after me. I am not worthy to stoop and loosen the thongs of his sandals. I have baptized your with water; he will baptize you with the Holy Spirit.'

| ◆ |

John the Baptist prefaces his preaching with the same words that Jesus will use: 'Repent'. St Peter in his second reading repeats the theme: 'The Lord does not delay his promise as some regard "delay", but he is patient with you, not wishing that any should perish but that all should come to repentance.'

There is a need for repentance and conversion because we should not live for this life only, because we look for the life of the world to come; and 'we await new heavens and a new earth'.

At the same time Mark emphasizes John the Baptist's role as subordinate to Christ. He will only baptize with water ('for repentance') whereas Jesus will baptize with the Holy Spirit.

John is the voice, but the Lord is the Word who was in the beginning. John is the voice that lasts for a time; from the beginning is the Word who lives for ever.

Take away the word, the meaning, and what is the voice? Where there is no understanding, there is only a meaningless sound. The voice without the word strikes the ear but does not build up the heart ... The voice of one crying in the desert is the voice of one breaking the silence. Prepare the way of the Lord, he says, as though he were saying: 'I speak out in order to lead him into your hearts, but he does not choose to come where I lead him unless you prepare the way for him.'

St Augustine, Sermon 293

St Augustine of Hippo (354–430)

St Augustine's mother, St Monica, was a Christian, but his father was a pagan. For thirty years he taught rhetoric and lectured. He also had a mistress and a child by her and fell under the influence of the Manichees. At length he moved to Milan and with the help of St Ambrose was baptized in 386. He returned to Africa in 388 and was ordained priest three years later, becoming Bishop of Hippo where he lived until his death. He is the first Christian biographer and produced the first best-seller *The City of God* which influenced thought for centuries. King Alfred translated his *Soliloquies* and many Orders used his *Rule*. His letters show that he was truly pastoral as well as possessing a unique theological mind.

| ♦ |

For joys of service, you we praise,
Whose favour crowneth all our days;
For humble tasks that bring delight,
When done, O Lord, as in your sight.
Accept our offerings, Lord most high,
Our work, our purpose sanctify,
And with our gifts may we have place,
Now in the Kingdom of your grace.
St Venantius Fortunatus (530–610)

Monday Second Week of Advent

Gospel: Luke 5:17–26

Jesus was teaching one day, and among the audience there were Pharisees and doctors of the Law who had come from every village in Galilee, from Judaea and from Jerusalem. And the Power of the Lord was behind his works of healing. Then some men appeared, carrying on a bed a paralysed man whom they were trying to bring in and lay down in front of him. But as the crowd made it impossible to find a way of getting him in, they went up on to the flat roof and lowered him and his stretcher down through the tiles into the middle of the gathering in front of Jesus. Seeing their faith Jesus said: 'My friend, your sins are forgiven you.' The scribes and the Pharisees began to think this over. 'Who is this man talking blasphemy? Who can forgive sins but God alone?' But Jesus, aware of their thoughts made them this reply, 'What are these thoughts you have in your hearts? Which of these is easier: to say, "Yours sins are forgiven you" or to say "Get up and walk"? But to prove to you that the Son of Man has authority on earth to forgive sins' – he said to the paralysed man – 'I order you: get up, and pick up your stretcher and go home.' And immediately before their very eyes he got up, picked up what he had been lying on and went home praising God.

| ♦ |

The prophecy of Isaiah talks of that Day when the Lord will come and the blind shall see and the lame shall leap like a deer.

St Luke places the healing of the paralytic after the healing of the leper and the call of Simon. Jesus clearly links his power to forgive sins (of God alone) with his healing of the paralytic. If he can do the latter, he can do the former. The people praised God as we should for that power of forgiveness given to his Church which brings about our freedom from the paralysis of our sins. Advent is a time to live in such a way that our lives reflect the gifts which God has given us.

The Father manifested his mercy by reconciling the world to himself in Christ, making peace by the blood of his Cross with all who are in heaven and on earth. The Son of God became man and lived among us so that he might free us from slavery to sin and call us out of darkness into his own wonderful light. Thus he commenced his work on earth by preaching repentance and saying: 'Repent and believe the Gospel' (Mark 1:15).

This invitation to penitence, which had often been issued by the prophets, prepared the hearts of the whole of humanity for the coming of the kingdom through the voice of John the Baptist who came preaching 'a baptism of repentance for the forgiveness of sins'.

But not only did Jesus exhort us to do penance, to give up our sins and be converted to God with all our hearts. He also received sinners and reconciled them to the Father. He cured the sick as a sign of his power to forgive sins. He himself even died for our sins and rose from the dead for our justification.

Introduction to the New Order of Penance,
Misericordiam Suam (1974) n. 1

| ♦ |

Lord Jesus Christ, who stretched out your hands on the Cross and redeemed us by your blood: forgive me, a sinner for none of my thoughts are hidden from you. Pardon I seek, pardon I hope for, pardon I trust to have. You who are full of pity and mercy: spare me, and forgive.

St Ambrose (339–397)

Tuesday Second Week of Advent

Gospel: Matthew 18:12–14

Jesus said to his disciples: 'Tell me. Suppose a man has a hundred sheep and one of them strays; will he not leave the ninety-nine on the hillside and go in search of the stray? I tell you solemnly, if he finds it, it gives him more joy than do the ninety-nine sheep that did not stray at all. Similarly, it is never the will of your Father in heaven that one of these little ones should be lost.'

| ♦ |

'He is like a shepherd feeding his flock, gathering lambs in his arms, holding them against his breast and leading to their rest the mother ewes.' So says Isaiah in a passage which records 'A voice cries, "Prepare in the wilderness a way for the Lord ..."'

One of the earliest depictions of Christ appears in the catacombs portraying Jesus as the Good Shepherd. Here he emphasizes that our Father in heaven is truly the Prodigal Father and his Son the one who seeks out and saves those who wander far from him. It is the mercy of God rather than his justice which is preached by the Church.

Lord Jesus Christ, who wishes none to perish, to whom all appeal with hope of mercy – for you said yourself: 'Whatever you ask the Father in my name, that I will do' – I beg of you in your name that in my dying moments you give me full use of my senses and speech; profound, heartfelt contrition for my sins; firm faith; hope in good measure and perfect love, that I may be able to say to you with a pure heart: 'Into your hands, O Lord, I commend my spirit. You have redeemed me, Lord God of truth, who are blessed and full of glory for ever and ever.' Amen.

Prayer of St Vincent Ferrer

St Vincent Ferrer (1350–1419)

Vincent was the son of an Englishman who had settled in Valencia. He became a Dominican in 1367. He spent his life preaching in Spain, France, Switzerland and Italy and was credited with many works of healing. He died at Vannes in France on 5 April. There was a spontaneous popular cult and he was canonized by Pius II in 1458.

| ♦ |

O merciful, almighty Father, you pour down your benefits upon us; forgive all our ingratitude. We have remained before you with dead, unfeeling hearts, not kindled with the love of your gentle and enduring goodness. Turn to us, O merciful Father and make us serve you alone with all of our heart.

St Anselm of Canterbury (1033–1109) – adapted

Wednesday Second Week of Advent

Gospel: Matthew 11:28–30

Jesus exclaimed: 'Come to me, all you who labour and are overburdened, and I will give you rest. Shoulder my yoke and learn from me, for I am gentle and humble in heart, and you will find rest for your souls. Yes, my yoke is easy and my burden is light.'

| ♦ |

After answering the disciples of John the Baptist, Matthew puts Jesus' reproaches of the towns of his ministry and then praises those who are truly childlike (Tuesday 1st Week of Advent).

The excerpt from the Gospel follows on from this. Isaiah says that the Lord 'gives strength to the wearied, he strengthens the powerless.' The Collect for the day asks that we may be not discouraged by our weaknesses. The appeal of Jesus to come to him and find rest comes from the heart of our merciful God. His yoke, compared with that of the scribes and Pharisees 'who impose on people burdens hard to carry [and] do not lift one finger to touch them' (Luke 11:46) is light indeed, because he is truly humble, and yet our mighty God.

Therefore the Lord Jesus took compassion on us in order that he might call us to himself and not scare us away. He comes as someone gentle, someone humble and then he says: 'Come to me all you who labour and I will refresh you' (Matthew 1:28). Thus the Lord Jesus refreshes. He neither excludes nor casts away. He rightly chose such disciples who, as messengers of the Lord's will, would gather together God's people, not disdain them.

St Ambrose, *On Penitence* I

St Ambrose (339–397)
He was the son of the Pretorian Prefect of Gaul and followed in his father's footsteps in the imperial service. In 370 he became governor of Aemilia and Liguria in Milan which was the capital of the Western Empire. On the death of the bishop in 374 the crowd acclaimed him (although he was not baptized) as the successor. He opposed the Arian heresy and reproved the Emperor for his military excesses (for which he did penance). He was in large part instrumental in the conversion of St Augustine.

| ♦ |

Humility always radiates the greatness and glory of God. How wonderful are the ways of God! He uses humility, smallness, helplessness and poverty to prove to the world that he loved the world.

Blessed Teresa of Calcutta (1910–1997)

Thursday Second Week of Advent

Gospel: Matthew 11:11–15

Jesus spoke to the crowds: 'I tell you solemnly, of all the children born of women, a greater than John the Baptist has never been seen; yet the least in the kingdom of heaven is greater than he is. Since John the Baptist came, up to this present time, the kingdom of heaven has been subjected to violence and the violent are taking it by storm. Because it was towards John that all the prophecies of the prophets and of the Law were leading; and he, if you will believe me, is the Elijah who was to return.

| ♦ |

At this point the liturgy introduces John the Baptist. Jesus pays tribute to his relative, saying that he is the greatest of the prophets because he was chosen to proclaim the Messiah and is in effect the Elijah who was to return.

But, as a cult of John the Baptist grew up in the early Church (cf. those who were baptized by John and knew nothing of the Holy Spirit – Acts 19:2) John is always portrayed as the 'friend of the bridegroom', and 'unworthy to undo the thong of Jesus' sandal'.

| ♦ |

The nature of John's preaching: 'You brood of vipers! Who warned you to flee from the coming wrath?' (Matthew 3:7) is more than hinted by Isaiah: 'See, I turn you into a thresh-ing-sled, new, with doubled teeth; you shall thresh and crush the mountains, and turn the hills to chaff. You shall winnow them and the wind will blow them away, the gale will scatter them.' The crowds poured out to listen to this excoriating message, yet in time John's disciples, encour-aged by John himself, followed by a growing throng, would rush to enter Jesus' kingdom. We belong to such an apos-tolic Church.

God established a time for his promises and a time for their fulfillment.

The time for promises was in the time of the prophets, until John the Baptist; from John until the end is the time of fulfillment.

God, who is faithful, put himself in our debt, not by receiving anything but by promising so much.

St Augustine: *Commentary on Psalm 109, 1*

St Augustine of Hippo (354–430)
Augustine's commentary on the Psalms dates from his time as Bishop of Hippo (396–430). They were probably taken down in writing from his preaching and then corrected for publication. For a fuller biography see under Second Sunday of Advent.

| ♦ |

Challenging and active John the Baptist stands before us, a 'type' of the manly vocation. In harsh terms he demands *metanoia*, a radical transformation of attitudes. Those who would be Christians must be 'transformed' ever again.

Pope Benedict XVI

Friday Second Week of Advent

Gospel: Matthew 11:16–19

Jesus spoke to the crowds: 'What description can I find for this generation? It is like children shouting to each other as they sit in the market place: "We played the pipes for you, and you wouldn't dance; we sang dirges, and you wouldn't be mourners."

For John came, neither eating, nor drinking, and they say, "He is possessed." The Son of Man came, eating and drinking, and they say, "Look, a glutton and a drunkard, a friend of tax collectors and sinners." Yet wisdom has been proved right by her actions.'

| ♦ |

This follows on from yesterday's Gospel. The messengers of John the Baptist have departed and Jesus takes the occasion to compare himself and John and the reception that both receive from the people.

Isaiah in the first reading says, 'I, the Lord, your God, teach you what is good for you, I lead you in the way that you must go.' John and Jesus were speaking the words of life, but the people, then as now could only see human characteristics. Isaiah goes on, 'If only you had been alert to my commandments, your happiness would have been like a river, your integrity like the waves of the sea.' If we want to hear God speaking to us, we must live in the way that Jesus taught, and free ourselves from human prejudices.

We should try to keep the mind in tranquillity. For the eye which is continually gazing about, at one time darting to one side and again to the other, frequently casting glances hither and thither, is not able to see clearly what is lying before it, but must fix its gaze firmly on that object, if a clear image is to be obtained. So, too, the human mind is incapable of perceiving the truth clearly, if it is distracted by innumerable worldly cares.

St Basil, *Letter* II

St Basil the Great (c.330–379)
Basil is virtually unique among saints in that his grandmother, mother, father, sister and brothers were all saints also. He was born in Caesarea and became a monk, settling near Neo-Caesarea in 358. Later as Bishop of Caesarea in 370, he gave his money to the poor and served out food himself to the hungry, and built a new town called Basiliad. Apart from his numerous theological writings he provided a rule which is followed by the majority of Eastern monastic congregations.

| ♦ |

Grant me, O Lord God, a watchful heart, which no curious thought will turn away from you; a noble heart, which no unworthy affection will drag down; a righteous heart, which no irregular intention will turn aside; a firm heart which no tribulation will crush; a free heart, which no violent affection will claim for its own.

St Thomas Aquinas (*c.*1225–1274)

Saturday Second Week of Advent

Gospel: Matthew 17:10–13

As they came down from the mountain the disciples put this question to Jesus, 'Why do the scribes say that Elijah has to come first?' 'True,' he replied; 'Elijah is to come to see that everything is once more as it should be; however I tell you that Elijah has come already and they did not recognize him but treated him as they pleased; and the Son of Man will suffer similarly at their hands.' Then the disciples understood that he had been speaking of John the Baptist.

| ♦ |

The Book of Ecclesiasticus (or Sirach) gives us one of the prophesies relating to the return of Elijah (the other is in Malachi). He represents the prophets, as Moses represents the Law. Both were seen with Jesus when he was transfigured on the mountain.

It was on their descent from the mountain that the disciples (under the impact of what they had seen) ask about the fulfilment of the prophecy. Jesus clearly names John as the Elijah who was to return (cf. Thursday 2nd Week of Advent). His role as witness to Jesus, is not just to be in words, but in his martyr's death. The Church has always recognized the role of John, giving him two feasts (his birth: June 24; and his martyrdom: August 29). The Basilica of St John Lateran, which is the Cathedral of Rome, is dedicated to St John the Baptist and St John the Evangelist.

There is no doubt that blessed John suffered imprisonment and chains as a witness to our Redeemer, whose forerunner he was, and gave his life for him. His persecutor had demanded not that he should deny Christ, but only that he should keep silent about the truth. Nevertheless, he died for Christ. Does Christ not say: 'I am the truth?' Therefore, because John shed his blood for the truth he surely died for Christ.

Through his birth, preaching and baptizing, he bore witness to the coming birth, preaching and baptism of Christ, and by his own suffering he showed that Christ also would suffer.

St Bede, *Homily 23*

St Bede, the Venerable (673–735)
Bede was a monk of Jarrow in the north east of England. He was ordained priest in 703 and wrote twenty-five books of scriptural commentaries as well as his famous *Ecclesiastical History of the English People*. Such was the public veneration that his remains were translated to Durham Cathedral. Pope Leo XIII named him a Doctor of the Church in 1899.

| ♦ |

May we always stand steadfast and without fear in every point of that faith which is taught by Christ's holy Catholic Church.

St John Fisher (1469–1535)

Third Sunday of Advent (Gaudete Sunday)*

Gospel: Luke 3:10–8 (C)

The crowds asked John the Baptist, 'What should we do?' He said to them in reply, 'Whoever has two cloaks should share with the person who has none. And whoever has food should do likewise.' Even tax collectors came to be baptized and they said to him, 'Teacher, what should we do?' He answered them, 'Stop collecting more than what is prescribed.' Soldiers also asked him, 'And what is it that we should do?' He told them, 'Do not practise extortion, do not falsely accuse anyone, and be satisfied with your wages.'

Now the people were filled with expectation, and all were asking in their hearts whether John might be the Christ. John answered them all, saying, 'I am baptizing you with water, but one mightier than I is coming. I am not worthy to loosen the thong of his sandals. He will baptize you with the Holy Spirit and fire. His winnowing fan is in his hand to clear his threshing floor and to gather the wheat into his barn, but the chaff he will burn with unquenchable fire.' Exhorting them in many other ways, he preached good news to the people.

| ♦ |

On this *Gaudete* (= Rejoice) Sunday, we are told by Isaiah 'Fear not, be not discouraged' and by St Paul 'Have no anxiety at all'. This is by way of calming any dread we may have of the Day of Judgement. John the Baptist clearly has that in mind when he uses the language of Isaiah referring to the winnowing fan and the threshing floor, where the chaff will be burnt up in unquenchable fire. It is as well to bear in mind that Jesus also talks in similar terms (Mark 9:48) of those who cause the little ones of God to sin.

We are also given a sample of John's spiritual direction. He

* Gaudete, from the first words of the Entrance Antiphon (Philippians 4:4)

is counselling perfection in many ways – expecting the soldiers to be content with their pay (notoriously late in coming and not very generous) and that tax collectors who made their living by commission should only collect what was prescribed. One can only imagine the queue at Zacchaeus' house after he said that he would repay four times over 'if I have extorted anything from anyone' (Luke 19:8). The request to share food and clothing would also perhaps have been received with a certain weary tolerance, rather as if he had asked a modern audience to cut down on their gambling. But we should not be too cynical. Change of heart does take place and in Advent we should examine whether we are living up to Christ's (and John's) standards rather than scaling down our standards to what the average worldly person expects.

———————— ♦ ————————

What then, does the Lord command as something new, as something proper to God, as the only thing which gives life, and not something which earlier failed to save? 'What does he point out?' What pre-eminent thing does he teach, he who as the Son of God is the new creature? He does not command what the letter says and what others have already done. He is asking for something greater, more divine, more perfect than that which is stated – that we denude the soul itself of its disordered passions, that we pull out by the roots and fling away what is foreign to the spirit. Here, then, is the teaching proper to a believer, and the doctrine worthy of the Saviour. Those, who before Christ's coming despised material goods, certainly gave up their riches and lost them, but the passions of the soul increased even more. For having believed that they had done something super-human, they came to indulge in pride, petulance, vainglory, despising others …

How much more fruitful is the opposite! On the one hand to own what is sufficient and not to be distressed by having to obtain it; and, on the other, to be able to help those in need.

Clement of Alexandria, *Who is the rich person who will be saved?* XI–XII

Clement of Alexandria (c.150–215)

Titus Flavius Clement was born in Athens but after his conversion to Christianity, travelled the world and reached Alexandria where he settled, and became Director of the School of Theology. During the persecution of Septimus Severus he fled to Cappadocia where he died.

| ♦ |

Make us, Lord, worthy to serve our brothers and sisters who are scattered all over the world, who live and die alone and poor. Give them today, using our hands, their daily bread. And, using our love, give them peace and happiness. Amen.

Blessed Teresa of Calcutta (1910–1997)

Monday Third Week of Advent

Gospel: Matthew 21:23–27

Jesus had gone into the Temple and was teaching, when the chief priest and the elders of the people came to him and said: 'John's baptism: where did it come from, heaven or man?' And they argued it out this way among themselves: 'If we say from heaven, he will retort: "Why then did you refuse to believe him?"; but if we say from man, we have the people to fear for they all hold that John was a prophet.' So their reply to Jesus was: 'We do not know.' And he retorted: 'Nor will I tell you my authority for acting like this ...'

| ♦ |

The reading from the Book of Numbers tells about the oracle of Balaam, who was not of Israel, but a Moabite, and, it would seem a soothsayer. Balaam is one of the most contradictory characters in the Bible because 'he acted willfully against the Lord.' It took a talking donkey to bring him to his senses and bless Israel instead of uttering a curse. He was destined to die in Moses' revenge raid on the Midianites.

In his oracle (we could hardly call it prophecy) he sees 'a star from Jacob takes the leadership, a scepter arises from Israel'. Unwittingly, his words receive sanction from God. In the same way John's baptism is given divine approval. In rejecting John, the scribes and Pharisees would in turn reject Jesus, because they could not admit that either of them possessed their authority from God.

The task of a prophet is to foretell future events, not to point them out. John is more than a prophet, because in his position as a precursor, he was indicating, pointing, to him whom he had prophesied about. But as he is neither a reed shaking in the wind, nor dressed in fine clothes, as the name 'prophet' is not enough to designate his title, let us listen to the way he should worthily be called: 'The Lord God says this: Look, I am going to send my messenger to prepare a way before me' (Malachi 3:1). What in Greek is expressed by the word *angel*, when translated means 'messenger'. It is justifiable, then, to call the one who has been sent to announce the Supreme Judge, an angel. For the name reflects the dignity of the action to be done. The name is certainly high ranking, but his life was not less inferior.

St Gregory I, *Homily on the Gospel* VI, 5

St Gregory the Great (c.540–604)
Forty of St Gregory's homilies on the Gospels have been preserved. He preached some to the Romans during the liturgical feasts of 591. For other biographical details see Saturday 1st Week of Advent.

| ♦ |

Let us draw near to this God, who has drawn near to us. In faith and trust, let us accept his authority over our lives and pray that his kingdom may extend over every nation and people.

Joseph A Mindling, OFM

Tuesday Third Week of Advent

Gospel: Matthew 21:28–32

Jesus said to the chief priests and the elders of the people: 'What is your opinion. A man had two sons. He went and said to the first: "My boy, you go and work in the vineyard today." He answered: "I will not go," but afterwards thought better of it and went. The man then went and said the same thing to the second who answered, "Certainly, sir," but did not go. Which of the two did the father's will?' 'The first,' they said. Jesus said to them, 'I tell you solemnly, tax collectors and prostitutes are making their way into the kingdom of God before you. For John came to you, a pattern of true righteousness, but you did not believe him, and yet the tax collectors and prostitutes did. Even after seeing that, you refused to think better of it and believe in him.'

| ♦ |

The crowd is always a bad judge of character. The crowd thought that John was possessed because he didn't drink. Yet he was a man of total integrity 'a pattern of true righteousness'.

Isaiah in his prophecy said that when the Day of the Lord comes 'I will leave a humble and lowly people'. It was only with such a disposition that Israel could listen to the message that God wanted to deliver. Such of course was Mary, Joseph ('a just man') Zechariah and Elizabeth ('Both were righteous in the eyes of God'), Simeon ('righteous and devout, awaiting the consolation of Israel') and Anna ('who worshipped night and day with fasting and prayer'). These all saw the Lord and believed in him.

Many live under obedience, more out of necessity than out of love of God, and they murmur and complain in their discontent. These will never achieve spiritual freedom until, for the love of God, they submit themselves with all their heart ...

It is indeed true that everyone likes to have his own way and is partial to those who think the same as he does. But if God dwells among us then we must sometimes relinquish our own opinion for the sake of peace. 'Who is so wise as to be able to know all things.' Therefore, rely not too heavily on your own opinion, but listen to the ideas of others as well. Your opinion may be a good one, but if, for God's sake you set it aside and follow that of another, you will profit the more.

Thomas a Kempis, *The Imitation of Christ*

Thomas a Kempis (1379–1471)

He was born in Kempen, near Dusseldorf. He asked to be admitted to the Canons Regular of St Augustine at Mount St Agnes outside Zwolle where his brother was prior. He took the name Thomas of Kempen (a Kempis *in Latin*) in 1399. He was ordained priest in 1413. He was elected sub-prior in 1425.

| ♦ |

The power of obedience! The lake of Genesareth had denied its fishes to Peter's nets. A whole night in vain. Then, obedient, he lowered his net again to the water and they caught 'a huge number of fish'. Believe me, the miracle is repeated every day.

St Josemaría Escrivá (1902–1975)

Wednesday Third Week of Advent

Gospel: Luke 7:19–23

John, summoning two of his disciples, sent them to the Lord to ask, 'Are you the one who is to come, or must we wait for someone else?' When the disciples of John the Baptist reached Jesus they said: 'John the Baptist has sent us to you, to ask: "Are you the one who is to come or have we to wait for someone else …?"' It was just then that he cured many people of diseases and afflictions and of evil spirits, and gave the gift of sight to many who were blind. Then he gave the messengers their answer, 'Go back and tell John what you have seen and heard: the blind see again, the lame walk, lepers are cleansed, and the deaf hear, the dead are raised to life, the Good News is proclaimed to the poor and happy is the man who does not lose faith in me.'

The prophecy of Isaiah would almost seem directed at the disciples of John the Baptist: 'Strengthen the hands that are feeble, make firm the knees that are weak, say to those whose hearts are frightened: Be strong, fear not!'

Jesus confirms them in their faith, by telling them that what they are witnessing is proof that he is the Messiah that their imprisoned master has been sent to announce to the people.

The time is at hand. The message is harsh: 'Here is your God, he comes with vindication; with divine recompense' (Isaiah) and 'Behold the Judge is standing before the gates' (St James). We must not forget that our loving Saviour will at the end be also the one who renders to each the reward of his or her works.

No doubt the Son of God in his omnipotence could have taught and sanctified us by appearing in a semblance of human form as he did to the patriarchs and prophets, when for instance he engaged in a wrestling context [with Jacob] or entered into conversation with them, or when he accepted their hospitality and even ate the food they set before him [Manoah and his wife, the parents of Samson]. But these appearances were only types, signs that mysteriously foretold the coming of one who would take a true human nature from the stock of the patriarchs who had gone before him. No mere figure then, fulfilled the mystery of our reconciliation with God, ordained from all eternity. The Holy Spirit had not yet come upon the Virgin nor had the power of the Most High overshadowed her, so that within her spotless womb Wisdom might build itself a house and the Word become flesh. The divine nature and the nature of a servant were to be united in one person so that the Creator of time might be born in time, and he through whom all things were made might be brought forth in their midst.

St Leo, *Letter* 31, 3

St Leo (d.461)
143 of St Leo's letters survive. In addition to his expressions of pastoral care, he writes about theological errors which surfaced at that time concerning the nature of the Incarnation. For further biographical details, see Tuesday 1st Week of Advent.

| ♦ |

Hold fast to Jesus, both in life and death, and trust yourself to his faithfulness, for he alone can aid you when all others fail.

The Imitation of Christ

Thursday Third Week of Advent

Gospel: Luke 7:24–30

When John's messengers had gone Jesus began to talk to the people about him: 'What did you go out into the wilderness to see?' A reed swaying in the breeze? No! Then what did you go out to see? A man dressed in fine clothes? Oh no, those who go in for fine clothes and live luxuriously are to be found at court! Then what did you go out to see? A prophet? Yes, I tell you, and much more than a prophet: he is the one of whom scripture says: See, I am going to send my messenger before you; he will prepare the way before you. I tell you, of all the children born of women, there is no greater than John: yet the least in the kingdom of God is greater than he is.' All the people who heard him, and the tax collectors too, acknowledged God's plan by accepting baptism from John; but by refusing baptism from him the Pharisees and the lawyers had thwarted what God had in mind for them.

| ♦ |

Jesus in the presence of John the Baptist's disciples continues his praise of their master. He comes in the same guise as the great prophets of old. He ironically asks whether the crowd have come to see a courtier, knowing the reputation of Herod (who would soon imprison John).

Jesus also draws attention to John's strength of character. He is no reed swaying to every wind of opinion. We are reminded of St Paul's 'Do I make my plans according to human considerations, so that with me it is "yes, yes" and "no, no"? As God is faithful, our word to you is not "yes" and "no". For the Son of God, Jesus Christ, who was proclaimed to you by us ... was not "yes" and "no" but "yes"' (1 Corinthians 1:17–20). John will remain firm even to his denunciation of Herod for openly flouting the commandments ('It is not lawful for you to have your brother's wife') and its consequence.

Wherefore he said: What did you go out into the wilderness to see? as though he had said, Why did you leave your cities, and your houses, and come together all of you into the wilderness, 'To see a pitiful and flexible kind of person?' So much people and so many cities would not have poured themselves out with so great zeal towards the wilderness and the river Jordan at that time, had you not expected to see some great and marvellous one, one firmer than any rock. It was not 'a reed' surely, that 'you went out to see shaken by the wind': for the flexible and such as are lightly brought round, and now say one thing, now another, and stand firm in nothing, are most like that.

St John Chrysostom, *Homily 27 on the Gospel*

St John Chrysostom (c.347–407)
He was the son of an army officer and became a monk in 373. He was ordained priest in 386 and became the bishop's special assistant and famous as a preacher. After the death of the Archbishop of Constantinople in 397, the Emperor wished him to be chosen in his place. He was consecrated in 398 but was banished several times as he had alienated the Empress. He eventually died in exile. He is considered in the East to be one of the Three Holy Hierarchs and Universal Teachers.

| ♦ |

It is easy to be consistent for a day or two. It is difficult and important to be consistent for one's whole life. It is easy to be consistent in the hour of enthusiasm; it is difficult to be so in the hour of tribulation. And only a consistency that lasts throughout the whole of life can be called faithfulness.

Pope John Paul II (1920–2005)

Friday Third Week of Advent

Gospel: John 5:33–36

Jesus said to the Jews: You sent messengers to John, and he gave his testimony to the truth: not that I depend on human testimony; no, it is for your salvation that I speak of this. John was a lamp alight and shining and for a time you were content to enjoy the light that he gave. But my testimony is greater than John's: the works my Father has given me to carry out, these same works of mine testify that the Father has sent me.

| ♦ |

John begins his Gospel by saying that John was sent by God 'to testify to the light, so that all might believe through him' (John 1:7). That light 'enlightens everyone'. We would call it the light of conscience which is in us all whether we ignore it or not.

Isaiah in the first reading refers to this when he says, 'Have a care for justice, act with integrity [and] blessed is the man who does this ... observing the Sabbath, not profaning it, and keeping his hand from every evil deed.' It is by our conduct that our truthfulness can be gauged.

Jesus appeals to the same principle, as he says on another occasion, 'If I do not perform my Father's works, do not believe me; but if I perform them, even if you do not believe me, believe the works so that you may realize that the Father is in me and I am in the Father' (John 10:37–39).

For by means of the creation itself, the Word reveals God the Creator, and by means of the world does he declare the Lord the Maker of the world; and by means of the formation [of man] the Artificer who formed him; and by the Son that Father who begat the Son; and these things do indeed address all mankind in the same manner, but all do not in the same way believe them. But by the law and the prophets did the Word preach both himself and the Father alike; and all the people heard him alike, but all did not alike believe. And through the Word himself who had been made visible and palpable, was the Father shown forth, although all did not equally believe in him; but all saw the Father in the Son: for the Father is the invisible reality of the Son, but the Son is the visible reality of the Father.

Anon, Letter to Diognetus

The anonymous author of the Letter addressed to Diognetus (i.e. to X) is a defence of the Christian lifestyle. It was probably written in Athens in the second century and may be part of the *Apologia* of Quadratus addressed to the Emperor Hadrian.

| ♦ |

I entreat you. O Lord, Holy Father, Everlasting God: Let your truth enlighten those of your servants who wander in doubt and uncertainty amid the darkness of this world; that their minds be opened, and that they may acknowledge you, the One God, the Father in the Son, and the Son in the Father, with the Holy Spirit, and enjoy the fruit of this confession, both here and in the life to come.

St Gregory the Great (c.540–604)

Fourth Sunday of Advent

Gospel: Matthew 1:18–24 (A)

This is how the birth of Jesus came about. When his mother Mary was betrothed to Joseph, but before they lived together, she was found with child through the Holy Spirit. Joseph her husband, since he was a righteous man, yet unwilling to expose her to shame, decided to divorce her quietly. Such was his intention when, behold, the angel of the Lord appeared to him in a dream and said, 'Joseph, son of David, do not be afraid to take Mary your wife into your home. For it is through the Holy Spirit that this child has been conceived in her. She will bear a son and you are to name him Jesus, because he will save his people from their sins.' All this took place to fulfil what the Lord had said through the prophet:

> Behold, the virgin shall conceive and bear a son,
> And they shall name him Emmanuel

which means 'God is with us'. When Joseph awoke, he did as the angel of the Lord had commanded him and took his wife into his home.

| ♦ |

At a time when Judah was threatened by the armies of Aram and Israel, Isaiah was sent to Ahaz, King of Judah to strengthen his faith and give him a sign that God was with him. The sign of the virgin with child has always been seen by the Fathers of the Church as a prophecy of the virgin birth of Jesus.

He is our Emmanuel who comes to abide with us, and at the end of his time on earth he will tell his disciples: 'Behold, *I am with you always*, until the end of the age' (Matthew 28:20). As Christmas draws near we need this sign for our faith.

The Lord himself has given us a sign here below on earth and in the heights of heaven, a sign that mankind did not request because it was never thought that such a thing would be possible. A virgin was with child and she bore a son who is called *Emmanuel*, which means 'God with us'. He came down to earth in search of the sheep that was lost, the sheep that was in fact his own creation, and then ascended to heaven above to offer to the Father and entrust to his care the human race that he had reclaimed.

St Irenaeus, *Against the Heresies* Book III, 19, 2

St Irenaeus (c.130–200)
He succeeded Photinus as Bishop of Lyons. He published his famous work *Against the Heresies* to refute the Gnostics and other heterodox opinions. In the peace that followed the persecution of Marcus Aurelius he visited his diocese and set about writing to confirm the faith of the faithful. In his famous work he defends the humanity of Jesus and his divinity, and how the whole of humanity is summed up in Him.

| ♦ |

May we bless and revere you, my Lady, O Virgin Mary, most holy Mother of God. You are in truth God's best creation; and no one has ever loved him so intimately as you, O glorious Lady.

St Bridget of Sweden (1303–1373)

17 December

Gospel: Matthew 1:1–17

A genealogy of Jesus, son of David, son of Abraham: Abraham was the father of Isaac, Isaac the father of Jacob, Jacob the father of Judah and his brothers, Judah was the father of Perez and Zerah, Tamar being their mother, Perez was the father of Hezron, Hezron the father of Ram, Ram was the father of Amminadab, Amminadab the father of Nahshon, Nahshon the father of Boaz, Rahab being his mother, Boaz was the father of Obed, Ruth being his mother, Obed was the father of Jesse; and Jesse was the father of King David.

David was the father of Solomon, whose mother had been Uriah's wife, Solomon was the father of Rehoboam, Rehoboam the father of Abijah, Abijah the father of Asa, Asa was the father of Jehoshaphat, Jehoshaphat the father of Joram, Joram the father of Azariah, Azariah was the father of Jotham, Jotham the father of Ahaz, Ahaz the father of Hezekiah, Hezekiah was the father of Manasseh, Manasseh the father of Amon, Amon the father of Josiah; and Josiah was the father of Jechoniah and his brothers. Then the deportation to Babylon took place.

After the deportation to Babylon: Jechoniah was the father of Shealtiel, Shealtiel the father of Zerubbabel, Zerubbabel was the father of Abiud, Abiud the father of Eliakim, Eliakim the father of Azor, Azor was the father of Zadok, Zadok the father of Achim, Achim the father of Eliud, Eliud was the father of Eleazar the father of Matthan, Matthan the father of Jacob; and Jacob was the father of Joseph the husband of Mary; of her was born Jesus who is called Christ.

The sum of generations is therefore: fourteen from Abraham to David; fourteen from David to the Babylonian deportation; and fourteen from the Babylonian deportation to Christ.

Genealogies attached a great importance to the Chosen People (we see how Zechariah belonged to the priestly division of *Abijah*). St Matthew traces Jesus' descent from Abraham down to Joseph, whereas St Luke goes from Joseph back to Adam (Luke 3:23–38).

Fourteen is twice seven (a perfect number) and in mystical Jewish writings this has a special significance. There is no need to consider those who have been omitted because the aim was to show descent from the key ancestors: Abraham, Isaac, Jacob, David, and Josiah.

Unusually the names of several women appear. These are not all righteous (Rahab for example) nor were they all Jewish (Tamar, Rahab and Ruth). It has been suggested that their inclusion was to indicate how that election by God was an anticipation of his later choice of a Virgin to be the Mother of his Son.

In his great love God intended the salvation of the entire human race. In preparation for this, in a special undertaking, he chose for himself a people to whom he would entrust his promises. By his covenant with Abraham and, through Moses, with the race of Israel, he acquired a people for himself, and to them he revealed himself in words and deeds as the one, true, living God. It was his plan that Israel might learn by experience God's way with humanity and by listening to the voice of God speaking to them through the prophets might gradually understand his ways more fully and more clearly, and make them more widely known among the nations ... and when the time had fully come the Word became flesh and dwelt among us, full of grace and truth. Christ established on earth the kingdom of God, revealed his Father and himself by deeds and words.

The Dogmatic Constitution on Divine Revelation:
Dei verbum promulgated at Vatican II
on 18 November 1965. nn. 14.17

| ♦ |

Father, all generation begins with you, and I thank you for loving us to the point of sending your Son to be one of us. Just as you prepared the world for his coming, prepare my heart that I may worthily receive him, and use me to bring him to others.

Joseph A. Mindling, OFM

18 December

Gospel: Matthew 1:18–24

This is how Jesus came to be born. His mother Mary was betrothed to Joseph, but before they came to live together she was found to be with child through the Holy Spirit. Her husband Joseph, being a man of honour and wanting to spare her publicity, decided to divorce her informally. He had made up his mind to do this when the angel of the Lord appeared to him in a dream an said, 'Joseph, son of David, do not be afraid to take Mary home as your wife, because she has conceived what is in her by the Holy Spirit. She will give birth to a son and you must name him Jesus, because he is the one who is to save his people from their sins.' Now all this took place to fulfil the words spoken by the Lord through the prophet:

> The virgin will conceive and give birth to a son and they will call him Emmanuel

A name which means 'God is with us'. When Joseph woke up he did what the angel of the Lord had told him to do: he took his wife to his home.

| ♦ |

It was because Joseph was 'a man of honour' we would say a just man, a man of righteousness, that he was attentive to the promptings of God, made known to him by the angel. Truly he fulfils the prophecy of Isaiah since he is of David's lineage, he is that virtuous branch for David. He takes Mary as his wife, even though he cannot fathom the mystery of her conception. He later will take the family to Egypt to save Jesus from the massacre of the Innocents.

Isaiah emphasizes the House of David, and the Messiah is that Branch 'who will reign as true king and be wise. He will bring home not just those of the nation only "but also", as Caiaphas prophesied, "to gather into one the dispersed children of God"' (John 11:52).

Hail Mary. Virgin and Handmaid. Virgin by the grace of him who was born of you without detriment to your virginity. Mother by reason of him you carried in your arms and suckled with your breast. Handmaid, because of him who took the form of a slave. The King entered your city, or to put it more clearly, into your womb; and later left as he wished, leaving your gates still closed. You have conceived as a virgin, and have given birth in a divine way.

Hail Mary, Temple in which God is received, or rather, holy Temple, as the prophet Davod exclaimed, 'Holy is your temple, admirable in goodness' (Psalm 65:4).

Hail Mary, most precious jewel of all the earth. Hail Mary, chaste dove. Hail Mary, the lamp always alight, for the Sun of Justice has been born of you.

St Cyril's *Homily* IV at the Council of Ephesus in 431

Cyril of Alexandria (c.376–444)
He was the nephew of Theophilus, the Patriarch of Alexandria, whom he succeeded in 412. He presided at the Council of Ephesus in 431 which proclaimed Mary, Mother of God. He was declared a Doctor of the Church by Leo XIII in 1882.

| ◆ |

O, that the soul of Mary were in us to glorify the Lord! That the spirit of Mary were in us to rejoice in God.

St Ambrose (339–397)

19 December

Gospel: Luke 1:5–25

In the days of King Herod of Judaea there lived a priest called Zechariah who belonged to the Abijah section of the priesthood, and he had a wife, Elizabeth by name, who was a descendant of Aaron. Both were worthy in the sight of God, and scrupulously observed all the commandments and observances of the Lord. But they were childless: Elizabeth was barren and they were both getting on in years.

Now it was the turn of Zechariah's section to serve and he was exercising his priestly office before God when it fell to him by lot, as the ritual custom was, to enter the Lord's sanctuary and burn incense there. And at the hour of incense the whole congregation was outside praying.

Then there appeared to him the angel of the Lord, standing on the right of the altar of incense. The sight disturbed Zechariah and he was overcome with fear. But the angel said to him, 'Zechariah, do not be afraid, your prayer has been heard. Your wife Elizabeth is to bear you a son and you must name him John. He will be your joy and delight and many will rejoice at his birth, for he will be great in the sight of the Lord; he must drink no wine, no strong drink. Even from his mother's womb he will be filled with the Holy Spirit, and he will bring back many of the sons of Israel to the Lord their God. With the spirit and power of Elijah he will go before him to turn the hearts of fathers towards their children and the disobedient back to the wisdom that the virtuous have, preparing for the Lord a people fit for him.' Zechariah said to the angel, 'How can I be sure of this? I am an old man and my wife is getting on in years.' The angel replied, 'I am Gabriel who stands in God's presence, and I have been sent to speak to you and bring you this good news. Listen! Since you have not believed my words, which will come true at their appointed time, you will be silenced and have no power of speech until this has happened.' Meanwhile the people were waiting for Zechariah and were surprised that he stayed in the sanctuary so long. When he came out he could not speak to them, and they realized that he had received a vision in the sanctuary. But he could only make signs to them, and remained dumb.

When his time of service came to an end he returned home. Some time later his wife Elizabeth conceived, and for five months she kept to herself. 'The Lord has done this for me,' she said, 'now that it has pleased him to take away the humiliation I suffered among men'.

| ♦ |

It was because Zechariah and Elizabeth were worthy in the sight of God and observed the commandments that they were chosen to be the parents of the one who would prepare the way for the Lord.

Zechariah had justifiable reasons for doubting the angel's message. He was old and his wife had born the humiliation of not giving birth to children. He was given time to reflect in the silence of his heart. The *Imitation of Christ* says, 'If you know how to suffer in silence, you will surely receive God's help.' It was to come true in Zechariah's case, and it will come true often in our own.

We are the true worshippers and true priests who, offering our prayer in the spirit, offer sacrifice in the spirit – that is, our prayer – as a victim that is appropriate and acceptable to God; this is what he has demanded and what he has fore-ordained for himself. This prayer, consecrated to him with our whole heart, nurtured by faith, prepared with truth; a prayer that is without blemish because of our innocence, clean because of our chastity; a prayer that has received the victor's crown because of our love for one another: this prayer we should bring to the altar of God with a display of good works amid the singing of psalms and hymns and it will obtain for us from God all that we ask. For what will God refuse to the prayer that comes to him from the spirit and in truth, since this is the prayer he has exacted?

Tertullian On Prayer, 28

Tertullian (c.155–230)

Quintus Septimus Florens Tertullianus was born in Carthage, the son of a centurion in 155. He became a Christian when he was thirty-eight and a champion of Christian faith. However towards the end of his life he adopted Montanist teachings and so is not considered one of the Fathers of the Church.

| ♦ |

Bestow on me, O Lord God, understanding to know you, diligence to seek you, wisdom to find you, a perseverance in waiting patiently for you, and a hope that may embrace you at the last.

St Catherine of Siena (c.1347–1380)

20 December

Gospel: Luke 1:26–38

The angel Gabriel was sent by God to a town in Galilee called Nazareth, to a virgin betrothed to a man named Joseph, of the House of David; and the virgin's name was Mary. He went in and said to her: 'Rejoice, so highly favoured! The Lord is with you.' She was deeply disturbed by these words and asked herself what this greeting could mean, but the angel said to her, 'Mary, do not be afraid; you have won God's favour. Listen! You are to conceive and bear a son, and you must name him Jesus. He will be great and will be called Son of the Most High. The Lord God will give him the throne of his ancestor David; he will rule over the House of Jacob for ever and his reign will have no end.' Mary said to the angel, 'But how can this come about, since I am a virgin?' 'The Holy Spirit will come upon you,' the angel answered, 'and the power of the Most High will cover you with its shadow. And so the child will be holy and will be called Son of God. Know this too: your kinswoman Elizabeth has, in her old age, herself conceived a son, and she whom people called barren is now in her sixth month, for nothing is impossible to God.' 'I am the handmaid of the Lord,' said Mary, 'let what you have said be done to me.' And the angel left her.

| ♦ |

St Luke contrasts and compares the visit of Gabriel to Zechariah and to Mary. Zechariah has what we would consider justifiable concerns: he is an old man and his wife is barren. He is silenced.

Mary on the other hand questions the angel but submits in faith, even though the implications were beyond human grasp: to bear a son who will rule forever over the House of Jacob and to sit on the throne of King David. So his mother prayed and meditated: 'and Mary kept all these things, reflecting on them in her heart' (Luke 2:20). Her acceptance brings about the real Advent, 'for the Word was made flesh and dwelt among us.' Faith will make demands of us, yet God, with our faith, will use us, as living stones to build his Church, with Mary our Mother as our intercessor and pattern of holiness.

———————— ◆ ————————

No one in the world has humbled herself as Mary has; so we may deduce that no one has been exalted as she has. It is in the measure of humility that God grants glory: He made her his mother, and who is going to compare our humility with hers? ... Our Lord, seeking to descend on earth, searched among all women, and selected only one: one who was beautiful beyond all others. He examined her in depth; all he found was humility and sincerity, good thoughts and a soul in love with God; a pure heart with desires of perfection. That is why God chose that pure soul and filled her with beauty. He descended from his seat on high and dwelt in blessedness among women; for there was no one on earth who could be compared with her. There was just one maiden, who was humble, pure, beautiful and immaculate, who was worthy to be his mother.

St James of Sarugh, *Homily on the Blessed Virgin, Mother of God*

St James of Sarugh (451–521)
He was born at Kurtam on the banks of the river Euphrates, (in modern day Syria). He became a monk at the age of twenty-two and in 519 was ordained bishop. He left many works, including several in verse and was called 'the flute of the Holy Spirit and the harp of the believing Church'.

| ◆ |

Our Lady was full of God because she lived for God alone, yet she thought of herself only as the handmaid of the Lord.

Blessed Teresa of Calcutta (1910–1997)

21 December

Mary set out and went as quickly as she could to a town in the hill country of Judah. She went into Zechariah's house and greeted Elizabeth. Now as soon as Elizabeth heard Mary's greeting, the child leapt in her womb and Elizabeth was filled with the Holy Spirit. She gave a loud cry and said, 'Of all women you are the most blessed, and blessed is the fruit of your womb. Why should I be honoured with a visit from the mother of my Lord? For the moment your greeting reached my ears, the child in my womb leapt for joy. Yes, blessed is she who believed that the promise made her by the Lord would be fulfilled.'

| ♦ |

It is commonly accepted that St John was filled with grace in the womb of Elizabeth. We should note the parallel with Samson, 'this boy is to be consecrated to God from the womb' (Judges 13:5). St Luke may have been a physician but he would not merely be commenting on gynaecological details. For him, this was the first encounter of the incarnate Word in the womb of Mary with the one who would be the *voice,* in the womb of Elizabeth.

There is also an obvious similarity between the barren mother (of John) and the virgin mother of Jesus who both give birth, because God looked upon their lowliness and blessed them. Elizabeth's greeting that Mary is, of all women the most blessed, is echoed by Jesus' words to Thomas, 'Blessed are those who have not seen *and have believed*' (John 20:29).

When the angel was announcing the mysteries to the Virgin Mary, he also told her, as a precedent to help her believe, that an old barren women had conceived. This is to show that God can do everything that pleases him.

When Mary heard this she hurried off to the hill country ... not because she disbelieved in his message, or was uncertain about the messenger, or doubted the precedent offered, but because she was overjoyed with desire, eager to fulfil a duty of piety and impelled by gladness.

Where could she that was filled with God hasten to, except to the heights ? There is no such thing as delay in the workings of the Holy Spirit. The arrival of Mary and the blessings of the Lord's presence are also speedily declared.

St Ambrose: *Treatise on the Gospel of St Luke*

St Ambrose (c.340–397)
Ambrose, who was born in Trier and was instrumental in the conversion of St Augustine, was renowned for his homilies. In particular his Treatise on St Luke, composed in 379 was an edited version of the homilies he gave to the people of Milan. For other biographical details see Wednesday 2nd Week of Advent.

| ♦ |

The ark of the covenant is incorruptible ... Joy at the Incarnation of the Word is an intrinsic part of our faith – the 'dancing in the presence of the ark' [2 Samuel 6:14]; the happiness: 'Blessed art thou among women and blessed is the fruit of thy womb, Jesus.'

Pope Benedict XVI

22 December

Gospel: Luke 1:46–56

Mary said: 'My soul proclaims the greatness of the Lord and my spirit exults in God my saviour; because he has looked upon his lowly handmaid. Yes, from this day forward all generations will call me blessed, for the Almighty has done great things for me. Holy is his name, and his mercy reaches from age to age for those who fear him.

'He has shown the power of his arm, he has routed the proud of heart. He has pulled down princes from their thrones and exalted the lowly. The hungry he has filled with good things, the rich sent empty away. He has come to the help of Israel his servant, mindful of his mercy – according to the promise made to our ancestors – of his mercy to Abraham and to his descendants for ever.'

Mary stayed with Elizabeth about three months and then went back home.

| ◆ |

Mary's canticle *The Magnificat* is in the tradition of the Psalms and the canticle in 1 Samuel 2:1–10 (which follows on from today's first reading) in which Hannah offers her son, Samuel, to God in the Temple: 'My heart exults in the Lord …'

Mary, in her turn will offer God's gift of his only Son to the Father, from Jesus' first miracle at Cana to his final offering on the Cross. We are privileged to make that same offering every time we come to Mass. In Advent we should ask Mary for that generosity of heart and fullness of faith to offer ourselves in union with her Son.

Blessed are you among all women, because without a seed you offered the fruit which will bless the whole earth, and will redeem it of the thorns of the curse.

Blessed are you among all women, because being a woman by nature, you will be the Mother of God. For, as he who will be born is the incarnate God, you will be called the Mother of God in your own right and out of merit, for it is God you are going to give birth to.

You carry God himself enclosed within your womb. He abides in you according to the flesh, and through you he presents himself as he had promised. He will obtain joy for all and he will transmit the divine light to the whole universe.

In you, O Virgin Mother, as in a pure and resplendent heaven, God 'placed his tabernacle; and he will come out of thee as the spouse from the bridal chamber' (Psalm 59:5–6).

St Sophronius, *Oration on the Annunciation of the Most Blessed Virgin Mary*

St Sophronius (c. 560–638)
St Sophronius was born in Damascus and became a monk in 580. He travelled extensively visiting monasteries in Egypt and in Rome. He became Patriarch of Jerusalem in 634 and died just as the city fell to the Moslems. He is the author of ten homilies and several Greek poems.

| ♦ |

What wonders O God, you have worked throughout the world.
All generations have shared the greatness of you love.
When you looked on Mary your lowly servant,
You raised her to be the mother of Jesus Christ, your Son our Lord, the saviour of all mankind.

from Preface of the Blessed Virgin Mary II

23 December

Gospel: Luke 1:57–66

The time came for Elizabeth to have her child and she gave birth to a son; and when her neighbours and relations heard that the Lord had shown her so great a kindness, they shared her joy.

Now on the eighth day they came to circumcise the child; they were going to call him Zechariah after his father, but his mother spoke up. 'No', she said 'he is to be called John.' They said to her, 'But no one in your family has that name', and made signs to his father to find out what he wanted him called. The father asked for a writing-tablet and wrote, 'His name is John'. And they were all astonished. At that instant his power of speech returned and he spoke and praised God. All their neighbours were filled with awe and the whole affair was talked about throughout the hill country of Judaea. All those who heard of it treasured it in their hearts. 'What will this child turn out to be?' they wondered. And indeed the hand of the Lord was with him.

| ♦ |

Zechariah had not revealed that part of the message about the naming of his son. At Jesus' circumcision he was given the name 'given him by the angel before he was conceived in the womb' (Luke 2:21). When the time came for John's circumcision, his father (who was obviously deaf and dumb) revealed the name (*John* means 'The Lord has shown his favour'), and immediately was freed of his impediment.

St Luke says 'he spoke and praised God' just as Mary proclaimed the greatness of God. John would be the messenger, who, in Malachi's words would prepare a way for the Lord, and be the Elijah that was promised.

John the Baptist is 'more than a prophet'. In him, the Holy Spirit concludes his speaking through the prophets. John completes the cycle of prophets begun by Elijah. He proclaims the imminence of the consolation of Israel; he is the 'voice' of the Consoler who is coming. As the Spirit of truth will also do, John 'came to bear witness to the light'. In John's sight, the Spirit thus brings to completion the careful search of the prophets and fulfils the longing of the angels. 'He on whom you see the Spirit descend and remain, this is he who baptizes with the Holy Spirit. And I have seen and have borne witness that this is the Son of God.

The Catechism of the Catholic Church *n*. 719.
– published by Pope John Paul II, on 11 October 1992;
the thirtieth anniversary of the opening of Vatican II.

| ♦ |

I pray my God that he will grant me perseverance and allow me to prove a faithful witness, right up to the time when I pass over to him, for my God's sake.

St Patrick (*c*.389–461)

24 December

Gospel: Luke 1:67–79

John's Father Zechariah was filled with the Holy Spirit and spoke this prophecy: 'Blessed be the Lord, the God of Israel, for he has visited his people, he has come to their rescue and he has raised up for us a power for salvation in the House of his servant David, even as he proclaimed, by the mouth of his holy prophets from ancient times, that he would save us from our enemies and from the hands of all who hate us. Thus he shows mercy to our ancestors, thus he remembers his holy covenant, the oath he swore to our father Abraham that he would grant us, free from fear, to be delivered from the hands of our enemies, to serve him in holiness and virtue in his presence, all our days. And you, little child, you shall be called Prophet of the Most High, for you will go before the Lord to prepare the way for him. To give his people knowledge of salvation through the forgiveness of their sins; this by the tender mercy of our God who from on high will bring the rising Sun to visit us, to give light to those who live in darkness and the shadow of death, and to guide our feet into the way of peace.'

| ♦ |

The *Benedictus* (which is part of the Church's Morning Prayer every day) draws also on the tradition of the Psalms. Zechariah would praise the fulfilment of the prophecy of Nathan to David that 'the Lord will make you a House … Your House and your sovereignty will always stand secure before me and your throne be established for ever.' God's promises are always fulfilled, but not necessarily in the way we would expect. The actual sovereignty of David would pass away but in its place would come the true king of creation. He would deliver us not just from any enemy, but from the enemy which is the burden of our sins.

You who are Christians, if you truly want to become one with him, remember whose bread it is that you eat, and thank him. You, yourself, when you have given someone a present, do you not expect him to thank you, and to bless the house from which that gift has come? And when you have not been thanked, how unappreciated you feel! Similarly, God patiently hopes that we will thank him for the food we have received from him, and that we will praise him when we are content with his gifts.

Accepting that we have received divine favours is a way of acknowledging them. If, on the other hand, when we receive them we keep quiet, and we forget about them through ingratitude or lacking in worthiness of such generosity, then we deprive ourselves of the opportunity for turning, in times of tribulation, to a God whose kindness we have not recognized ...

St Maximus of Turin, *Homily* 72, 3

St Maximus of Turin (c.380–65)
He became the first known Bishop of Turin in 398. A hundred of his homilies have been preserved. He urged the importance of prayer to obtain God's grace and a committed practice of the faith to convert the unbelievers.

| ♦ |

Almighty, most holy, most high and supreme God, holy and just Father, Lord King of heaven and earth, for yourself we give thanks to you because by your holy will, and by your only son, you have created all things.

St Francis of Assisi (1181–1226)

Christmas (Midnight)

Gospel: Luke 2:1–15

In those days a decree went out from Caesar Augustus that the whole world should be enrolled. This was the first enrollment when Quirinius was governor of Syria. So all went to be enrolled, each to his own town. And Joseph too went up from Galilee from the town of Nazareth to Judaea, to the city of David that is called Bethlehem, because he was of the house and family of David, to be enrolled with Mary, his betrothed, who was with child. While they were there, the time came for her to have her child, and she gave birth to her first-born son. She wrapped him in swaddling clothes and laid him in a manger, because there was no room for them in the inn.

Now there were shepherds in that region living in the fields and keeping the night watch over their flock. The angel of the Lord appeared to them and the glory of the Lord shone around them and they were struck with fear. The angel said to them, 'Do not be afraid: for behold, I proclaim to you good news of great joy that will be for all the people. For today in the city of David a saviour has been born for you who is Christ and Lord. And this will be a sign for you: you will find an infant wrapped in swaddling clothes and lying in a manger.' And suddenly there was a multitude of the heavenly host with the angel, praising God and saying:

> Glory to God in the highest and on earth peace to those on whom his favour rests.

| ♦ |

St Luke is anxious to fix the birth of Christ in its historical context (around 6BC). But he also wants to draw a dramatic contrast. On one side are the earthly powers who decide the lives of their subjects. On the other is the King of Kings born in a stable who is revealed to the poorest inhabitants of the Roman empire – for both, a Saviour has been born.

Such a birth, my beloved, was fitting for the strength and wisdom of God, who is Christ, so that in him, there was a similarity to us through humanity, and we were given the advantage of his divinity. If he were not God, he would not be able to offer a remedy. If he were not man, he would not have been able to give us an example. This is why the angels announced, singing joyfully: Glory to God in the highest, and proclaiming: Peace on earth to men of good-will. They see that the heavenly Jerusalem is being raised up in the midst of the nations of the world. What joy this ineffable work of divine goodness should cause in the little world we inhabit, if such joy is caused in the sublime sphere of the angels! ... O Christian, recognize your dignity, for you share in the divine nature.

St Leo I, *Homily on the Nativity* I

St Leo the Great (d. 461)
Ninety-two homilies of St Leo (which he preached on the principal feasts of the liturgical year) have been preserved. Biographical details can be found on Tuesday 1st Week of Advent.

| ♦ |

We were the cause of the Word of God taking human form. In his great love he was born and took flesh for our salvation.

St Athanasius (c.296–373)

Christmas (Dawn)

Gospel: Luke 2:15–20

When the angels went away from them to heaven, the shepherds said to one another: 'Let us go then, to Bethlehem to see this thing that has taken place, which the Lord has made known to us.' So they went in haste and found Mary and Joseph, and the infant lying in the manger. When they saw this, they made known the message that had been told them about this child. All who heard it were amazed by what had been told them by the shepherds. And Mary kept all these things, reflecting on them in her heart. Then the shepherds returned, glorifying and praising God for all they had heard and seen, just as it had been told to them.

| ♦ |

It is no accident that the first message of the Saviour's birth would be brought to those who were *outside* in the fields. The shepherds were physically and spiritually the poor and despised of Israel.

To them the angel gave the news that the prophecy of Isaiah was being fulfilled: they were part of God's holy people, the redeemed of the Lord and no longer to be called forsaken. St Paul comments, 'not because of any righteous deeds we had done but because of his mercy' (second reading).

The shepherds trusted in the angel's message 'that the Lord has made known to us'. Their reward was to see the love of God made visible in his own Son.

He was wrapped up in swaddling clothes; but at his resurrection he cast away the cloths in the sepulchre.

He lay in a manger, but later he was feted by the angels, pointed to by a star and adored by the wise men.

Why do you marvel at what you have seen with your eyes, while you do not observe what is perceived by the mind and the heart?

St Gregory Nazianzen, Oration 29,19

St Gregory Nazianzen (329–389)
Gregory studied at the University of Athens with Basil the Great and the future Emperor, Julian ('the Apostate'). He then left to pursue a solitary life with Basil in Pontus. He was ordained priest in 361 and later was consecrated Bishop of Sasima. He played an important part in the Council of Constantinople in 381 and subsequently was appointed Bishop of Constantinople with his throne in Santa Sophia. He is one of the four Eastern Doctors of the Church and because of his outstanding teaching is known as 'The Theologian'.

| ♦ |

We hold as a gift more precious than gold, your love. From the beginning of creation your Son, the eternal Word, has been tossing about on the stormy waters of human souls, striving to bring peace through the gift of love. Now he has breathed over the waters of our souls, and the waves are calm. Merciful Father, we thank you.

Blessed William of Saint Thierry (1085–1148)

Christmas Day

Gospel: John 1:1–18

In the beginning was the Word, and the Word was with God, and the Word was God. He was in the beginning with God. All things came to be through him, and without him nothing came to be. What came to be through him was life, and this life was the light of the human race; the light shines in the darkness, and the darkness has not overcome it.

A man named John was sent from God. He came for testimony, to testify to the light, so that all might believe through him. He was not the light, but came to testify to the light. The true light, which enlightens everyone, was coming into the world. He was in the world, and the world came to be through him, but the world did not know him. He came to his own, but his own people did not accept him. But to those who did accept him he gave power to become children of God, to those who believe in his name, who were born not by natural generation nor by human choice nor by a man's decision but of God. And the word became flesh and made his dwelling among us, and we saw his glory, the glory as of the Father's only son, full of grace and truth.

John testified to him and cried out, saying, 'this was he of whom I said, "The one who is coming after me ranks ahead of me because he existed before me."' From his fullness we have all received, grace in place of grace, because while the law was given through Moses, grace and truth came through Jesus Christ. No one has ever seen God. The only Son, God, who is at the Father's side, has revealed him.

| ♦ |

St John gives us a profound meditation on the coming of Jesus into the world. Unlike the other Evangelists he does not begin with history, but contemplates Jesus as the Word, existing from all time with the Father, but through whom all things come to be.

In the second reading, the Letter to the Hebrews speaks

to us of the Son 'whom he made heir of all things and through whom he created the universe, who is the refulgence of his glory, the very imprint of his being, and who sustains all things by his mighty word.'

That Word is the true light which enlightens. He is the very mind of God that gives meaning to humanity. We can no longer say that God does not understand us, because He has become one of us. The light of his coming has penetrated our darkness, which Benedict XVI has said is like living in a tunnel, an underpass of arid secularism. God makes his presence felt and his light shine out from the morning watch even unto night, so that he could give power to those who believe in him, to become children of God.

---------- ◆ ----------

This is the mystery which we celebrate, that the light has come into the world and has given it light when it was shrouded in darkness, and that the day-spring has visited us from on high and given light to those who were sitting in darkness ... The true light which enlightens everyone coming into this world, has come. Let us all be enlightened, let us all be filled with light. Let none of us remain a stranger to this brightness. Let no one who is filled with it continue in the darkness. But let us all go forth shining with light.

St Sophronius, *Oration* 3, 6

St Sophronius (c.560–638)
St Sophronius opposed the heresy of the Monothelites. He emphasized the true nature of the Incarnation and incurred much suffering for his defence of the faith. Other biographical details can be seen on 22nd December.

| ◆ |

Of the Father's love begotten, ere the worlds began to be,
He is Alpha and Omega, He the source, the ending he,
Of the things that are, that have been,
And that future years shall see. Evermore and evermore.
Marcus Aurelius Prudentius (348–413) *Corde Natus ex Parentis*

Second Sunday after Christmas:
The Holy Family

Gospel: Luke 2:22–40 (B)

When the days were completed for their purification according to the Law of Moses, they took him up to Jerusalem to present him to the Lord, just as it is written in the law of the Lord, 'Every male that opens the womb shall be consecrated to the Lord', and to offer the sacrifice of 'a pair of turtledoves or two young pigeons', in accordance with the dictate in the law of the Lord.

Now there was a man in Jerusalem whose name was Simeon. This man was righteous and devout, awaiting the consolation of Israel, and the Holy Spirit was upon him. It had been revealed to him by the Holy Spirit that he should not see death before he had seen the Christ of the Lord. He came in the Spirit into the temple and when the parents brought in the child Jesus to perform the custom of the law in regard to him, he took him into his arms and blessed God, saying: 'Now Master, you may let your servant go in peace, according to your word, for my eyes have seen your salvation, which you prepared in sight of all the people, a light for revelation to the Gentiles, and glory for your people Israel.'

The child's father and mother were amazed at what was said about him; and Simenon blessed them and said to Mary his mother, 'Behold, this child is destined for the fall and rise of many in Israel, and to be a sign that will be contradicted – and you yourself a sword will pierce – so that the thoughts of many may be revealed.' There was also a prophetess, Anna, the daughter of Phanuel, of the tribe of Asher. She was advanced in years, having lived seven years with her husband after her marriage, and then as a widow until she was eighty-four. She never left the temple, but worshipped night and day with fasting and prayer. And coming forward at that very time, she gave thanks to God and spoke about the child to all who were awaiting the redemption of Jerusalem.

When they had fulfilled all the prescription of the law of the Lord, they returned to Galilee, to their own town of Nazareth. The child grew and became strong, filled with wisdom; and the favour of God was upon him.

| ◆ |

Children are always a gift from God. The birth of his son, Isaac, was God's answer to Abraham, our father in faith.

At the heart of the Gospel we find those who were faithful to God, fulfilling the commands of the law. Mary presents her first-born child to God, because in truth 'he belonged to Him' (Exodus 13:2). We need to regard each child with that reverence which God gives and value the love and respect which should be at the centre of family life.

––––––––––– ◆ –––––––––––

The prophets, who receive the gift of prophecy from the Word of God foretold his coming in the flesh, which accomplished the union and communion between God and man which was predetermined by the Father ... From the beginning the Word of God prophesied that God would be seen by mankind and he would live on earth and speak with his own creation, bringing salvation and made visible and present among them.

St Irenaeus, *Against the Heresies* 4, 20

St Irenaeus of Lyons (c. 130–200)
A disciple of Polycarp, Bishop of Smyrna, he studied in Rome and became a priest of Lyons. He succeeded Bishop Pothinus in 178. He was an effective peacemaker but is known for his principal works, *The Demonstration of Apostolic Preaching* and *Against the Heresies*. He emphasized the identity of the God of the Old Testament and that of the New and the unity of the Father and the Son in the work of redemption.

| ◆ |

Let us ask Our Lady and St Joseph to make our families what they made Nazareth for Jesus ... Love does not live on words, nor can it be explained by words – above all that love which serves him and comes from him and which finds him, touches him, serves him, loves him in others. As the Father has loved his Son, so he has loved us, and loves us now.

Blessed Teresa of Calcutta (1910–1997)

Mary, Mother of God (1 January)

Gospel: Luke 2:16–21

The shepherds went in haste to Bethlehem and found Mary and Joseph, and the infant lying in the manger. When they saw this, they made known the message that had been told them about this child. All who heard it were amazed by what had been told them by the shepherds. And Mary kept all these things, reflecting on them in her heart. Then the shepherds returned, glorifying and praising God for all they had heard and seen, just as it had been told to them. When eight days were completed for his circumcision, he was named Jesus, the name given him by the angel before he was conceived in the womb.

| ♦ |

One of the most ancient feasts of Our Lady has replaced the previous feast of the Circumcision of Jesus (but retaining the reference in the Gospel). Jesus is born subject to the law of Moses, and is born 'of a woman, under the law, to ransom those under the law' (2nd reading).

But Mary, unlike the shepherds who cannot stop speaking about what they had seen and heard, meditates in silence on the impact of what had taken place and the part she had played and would play ever after. May she pray for us throughout the coming year, and help us to hear the word of God and keep it (Luke 11:28).

The title of Mary as our mother is not merely symbolic. Mary is our mother in the most real and lofty sense, a sense which surpasses that of earthly maternity. She has brought forth our life of grace for us because she offered up her entire being, body and soul, as the Mother of God.

St Teresa Benedicta of the Cross

St Teresa Benedicta of the Cross (1891–1942)
Edith Stein was born of Jewish parents in Breslau (now Wroclaw). She studied philosophy at university and worked as a nurse during the First World War. In 1933 she entered the Carmelites in Cologne and took the name Teresa Benedicta of the Cross. She was arrested in 1942 by the Nazis, with her sister, Rosa and sent to Auschwitz where they died in the gas chamber. She was canonized in 1998 and was made a patron of Europe by John Paul II.

| ♦ |

During this time of grace let us, in a special way, ask our Lady to teach us her silence, her kindness and her humility.

Silence of Mary speak to me, teach me how with you and like you I can learn to keep all things in my heart as you did ... to pray always in the silence of your heart as you did.

Blessed Teresa of Calcutta (1910–1997)

Epiphany of the Lord

Gospel: Matthew 2:1–12

When Jesus was born in Bethlehem of Judaea, in the days of King Herod, behold, magi from the east arrived in Jerusalem, saying, 'Where is the newborn king of the Jews? We saw his star at its rising and have come to do him homage.' When King Herod heard this, he was greatly troubled, and all Jerusalem with him. Assembling all the chief priests and the scribes of the people, he inquired of them where the Christ was to be born. They said to him, 'In Bethlehem of Judaea, for thus it has been written through the prophet:

> And you, Bethlehem, land of Judah, are by no means least among the rulers of Judah;
> Since from you shall come a ruler, who is to shepherd my people Israel.'

Then Herod called the magi secretly and ascertained from them the time of the star's appearance. He sent them to Bethlehem and said, 'Go and search diligently for the child. When you have found him, bring me word, that I too may go and do him homage.' After their audience with the king they set out. And behold, the star that they had seen at its rising preceded them, until it came and stopped over the place where the child was. They were overjoyed at seeing the star, and on entering the house they saw the child with Mary his mother. They prostrated themselves and did him homage. Then they opened their treasures and offered him gifts of gold, frankincense and myrrh. And having been warned in a dream not to return to Herod, they departed for their country by another way.

| ♦ |

We rightly see in the homage of the magi, the fulfilment of Isaiah's prophecy (Isaiah 60:1–6), that the nations will come from afar ('bearing gold and frankincense and myrrh') to the Messiah-King of Israel. Countless gifts have followed:

from the alabaster jar of perfume to the tribute given by 'every tribe and tongue and people and nation' in great generosity and in holiness of life.

The wise men 'enter the house' and adore their king; as we should, each time we enter the house of God and dwelling-place of the Most High. We should also ask him to accept our gifts of bread and wine 'for the praise and glory of his name, for our good and the good of all his Church.'

————————◆————————

The magi follow the star and reach a child, the Lord Jesus Christ. They see him in the flesh and they adore the Word; they see him a child and worship Wisdom; they see weakness and understand his Power: that he is the Lord of Majesty.

In witness to their faith and wisdom they offer gifts from the heart. A gift of frankincense to the God; myrrh to the Man, gold to the King. They venerate at the same time the divine and the human nature in an undivided unity.

St Leo I, *Homily 3 on the Epiphany of the Lord*

Leo I (d. 461)
He became Pope in 440. His statement at the Council of Chalcedon in 451 on the Incarnation was acclaimed as masterly. His homilies on the principal liturgical feasts have that same theological precision which praises the humanity and divinity of Jesus.

| ◆ |

Lord, I desire to offer myself to you freely and for ever. I give myself to you this day with a sincere heart, to serve you in obedience and as a sacrifice of endless praise. Accept me today, together with this holy sacrifice of your precious Body, which I offer you in the presence of the unseen choirs of angels, who wait on you in heaven. May it be for my salvation and that of all your holy Church.

The Imitation of Christ

Sources

The Scripture quotations for weekdays are taken from *The Jerusalem Bible* version © 1966, 1967, 1968 Darton Longman & Todd, and Doubleday & Co Inc.. The Sunday quotations are from *The New American Bible* © 1970 The Confraternity of Christian Doctrine, Washington D.C.

The quotations from Pope Benedict XVI are taken from *Co-Workers of the Truth* translated by Sister Francis McCarthy and Reverend Lothar Krauth © 1992 Ignatius Press, San Francisco.

The *Sayings of Mother Teresa* are from *Jesus, the Word to be spoken* (compiled by Fr Angelo Scolozzi) Claretian Publications ©1999 Bangalore.

The Prayers of St Anselm, St Thomas Aquinas, St Benedict, St Catherine of Siena, St Vincent Ferrer, St Francis of Assisi, St Gregory the Great and St William of Thierry are taken from *At Prayer with the Saints* compiled by Anthony F. Chiffolo © 1998 Liguori, Missouri.

Matthew, A Devotional Commentary (General Editor Leo Zanchettin) is published by The Word among us© 1997 Ijamsville.

The homily of Pope John Paul (Mexico City, 27 January 1979) is taken from *L'Osservatore Romano*.

The quotation from St John Chrysostom is taken from *The Saving Word. Year A.* © 1981 Michael Glazier, Delaware and Dominican Publications, Dublin.

The quotations from St Josemaría Escrivá are taken from *The Way* © 1985 Scriptor S.A.